SOS
VENEZUELA

Original title: SOS Venezuela

Published by Editorial Alfa
C. Centre, 5. Gavà 08850. Barcelona, España
e-mail: contacto@alfadigital.es
www.alfadigital.es

ISBN 978-84-17014-18-6 (Paperback Edition)
ISBN 978-84-17014-19-3 (Ebook Edition)

Editing by Magaly Pérez Campos
Translation by Joshua Farley
Translation review by Maryflor Suárez
Book design by Ulises Milla
Author photo by Jessica Naranjo

First printing edition 2018
Printed by Amazon.

SOS
VENEZUELA
A BRIEF STORY
OF A WRECKED COUNTRY
LAUREANO
MÁRQUEZ

TRANSLATED BY JOSHUA FARLEY

60*th.*
aniversary
Editorial **Alfa**
1958 - 2018

To Laura, my daughter. With all my love,
my little grain of sand for the free Venezuela
I dream of for you.

Contents

Preface

It may seem to the English-speaking reader that Venezuela is a remote country both geographically and, above all, politically, a country which has become a hot topic of discussion in recent times without it being entirely understood what is going on over there: is it a dictatorship? A dictator elected by the voters? Is such a thing possible?

Venezuela particularly stands out due to an issue that carries great weight in the first world: the severe human rights violations produced in the country and the frantic way in which widening crowds of Venezuelans are fleeing from their homeland, many times by walking straight through the borders of neighboring countries. As once stated by the Cuban poet José Martí, "when people emigrate, the rulers abound."

Venezuela has become a failed state. The populist demagogy, which has led what is considered to be one of the wealthiest countries on the American continent to ruin, should not come off as a surprise to developed countries where, with other styles and characteristics but a similar recklessness, it's perfectly reasonable that a model instilled on the basis of popular vote could eventually end up bringing about the eradication of democratic principles and freedom. Democracy, which is currently inexistent in Venezuela, is likewise threatened in such critical countries as the United States of America and the United Kingdom, where we have also seen these principles cave in under the weight of the manipulated emotions generated by popular discontent. On occasion, the leaders of free and open societies can awaken the most authoritarian and narrow-minded sides in the people.

In this book, we are going to describe to you how the aforementioned process of emotional and political manipulation, which employed democracy in order to effectively end democracy, was produced in Venezuela. We boasted the most resilient democracy on the continent and, with its imperfections, gave rise to the greatest period of progress, peace, stability, and tolerance that Venezuela has ever seen.

First off, we shall conduct a quick run-through of our past to place the reader in the context of the crisis we are facing, as well as our deepest roots. What is happening in today's Venezuela is not an isolated occurrence; on the contrary, we must examine some of the greatest evils that have marked our historical timeline: *caudillismo*, militarism, profit-seeking for capitalist gain, and much more.

Secondly, we shall introduce a description of the political regime in Venezuela that has come to be known as "Chavism" and which celebrates its twentieth year in power in December 2018. To this effect, we shall recount a brief story of how the democratic institutions were overridden by making use of the popular vote (as well as fear, fraud, and threats) to bestow an increasing amount of power and discretion to the *caudillo*.

We shall denominate the administration of Hugo Chávez as the *soft dictatorship* because it represented the transition from democracy to dictatorship, a transition by means of which democratic institutions were progressively dismantled and eliminated. By the time Chávez passed away while still governing the country, Venezuelan democracy was already an empty shell.

With his successor, Nicolás Maduro, the *hard dictatorship* was consolidated in all its destructive cruelty, not only of lives—which is bad enough as is—but also of the productive apparatus through economic policies that led the country to the most extravagant currency devaluation on the planet and resulted in all kinds of calamities among the population.

We wanted to present this first English version of *SOS Venezuela* as more than just a call to alarm so that the world won't forget about us during this dreadful moment in which international observation and action on behalf of multilateral organizations in charge of ensuring respect for human rights serve as our only aid so that the Venezuelan regime mitigates, at the very least, the total impunity it displays in its diverse final judgments. These brief pages also intend to raise alarm regarding the phenomenon of *anti-politics* that is being spread so strongly throughout Western democracies. This trend, whereby some claim to represent a nation's true values and the monopoly on patriotism for themselves, is extremely dangerous because it implicitly carries the seed of authoritarianism and dictatorship, considering anyone who doesn't share said mentality and who rejects such designs as a traitor.

Perhaps it would be necessary to make known to the reader that the author of these pages is essentially known in Venezuela for his activity as a humorist. Humor always acts as a keen manifestation of the intellect that helps us understand the great sufferings of mankind, attempts to find some explanation to modify them, and gives us hope to survive. However, this is not a humor book. This time, the circumstances demand that the reality of our human catastrophe be told in all its harshness so that it may be understood.

Venezuela is a land of good, hard-working people, as well as landscapes of extraordinary beauty. We merit a better destiny and we are currently fighting to regain democracy and freedom. The potential concern shown by the readers will be of great help both to us and to them, even if they may not believe so at first. At the end of the day, the struggle for democracy is not the matter of a single country, no matter how remote it may seem to us. Regardless of where freedom succumbs, all of humanity will be brought down with it.

LAUREANO MÁRQUEZ

Introduction

Venezuela is coursing through one of the most complicated periods of its history. The nation's survival is threatened by a lack of food, medicine, and basic items, violence, and, above all, the limitless greed for power which has transformed a traditionally democratic society into the victim of a regime that acts outside the boundaries of constitutional order and has been sanctioned on an international level for crimes including administrative incompetence, corruption, human rights violations, ties with terrorism, and drug trafficking. The panorama couldn't be more disheartening. The illusion of well-being that Chávez created in Venezuelans ended up collapsing into a resounding failure.

The purpose of this book is to explain, briefly and schematically to the reader curious to know what is going on in Venezuela, a sequence of events that is difficult even for us Venezuelans to understand, and we are the ones suffering from them. At times, we are even forced to ask ourselves how we reached such a conflicting moment in our history. This book also aims to act as a warning, based on our arduous experiences, of the effects that demagogic populism has on the people, of how much leaps of faith prove to be unpredictable in politics, and of how counterproductive is the foolish belief that projects for change may be built based on the premise that "we've already hit rock bottom and it can't get any worse." Venezuela is proof that a country with magnificent potential may encounter no restraints in its downfall.

The anti-politics message that decimated Venezuela has caught attention all over the world—even in developed countries with an extensive institutional tradition—because it simplifies reality and we are living in times of simplification, of 140-character theories, of virtual networks that often substitute reality.

There is a need to rekindle certain principles and values which form the basis of our lives, and politics is one of these. To this effect, we wish to situate the idea of politics as a noble task, a civil duty, a commitment to love and solidarity for the fellow human being. Power is not an end in its own right; its purpose is to serve human beings and their happiness.

In these pages, we will explore a brief summary of Venezuela's history, thereby allowing the readers to place themselves in the remote origin of the evils that haunt Venezuela today. We will also recap the birth of Chavism at the hand of its founder, Hugo Chávez, who set the stage for the confiscation of freedoms which has led us to the crisis in which the Venezuelan democracy currently finds itself suffering. Without that "soft" dictatorship, the subsequent "hard" dictatorship would not have been possible.[1]

This book is also a cry for help, not only a cry for food and medical supplies. We need help

---

1 The terms "soft" and "hard" dictatorship originate from a pun on the Spanish word *dictadura*, meaning "dictatorship." Whereas *blanda* means "soft" and *dura* means "hard," *dicta-blanda* refers to the "soft" dictatorship of Hugo Chávez and *dicta-dura*, in this case, refers to the "hard" dictatorship of Nicolás Maduro.

to attain freedom. One of the standing themes since the founding of the United Nations is how to ensure that the people mutually support one another in the defense of democratic values, as well as to ensure that international law takes precedence over the law of the strongest or most heavily armed, otherwise we would be repeating on a global scale what goes on within authoritarian regimes. Part of this support is to create global awareness for civil solidarity so that international bodies don't end up reacting too late in the face of political tragedies that almost always end with a great number of innocent people losing their lives in exchange for a more just, accepting, and democratic existence for the rest.

The author of these pages—which have turned out way too serious—is a humorist by profession in Venezuela. Over the past 18 years I have tried to give warning, by means of my humor, regarding the grave threat being woven against freedom and democracy. Oftentimes, it is up to humor to say the things that others cannot or will not dare to say. This is not a humor book, however, but rather a reflexive attempt to synthesize a set of historical and political circumstances that drove my country into the terrible situation which torments it today.

As Venezuelans, we will escape from this crisis. Aside from the hardships we relate to you, my dear readers, we would be delighted for you to fall in love with our land, to fall in love with its light, its landscapes, its beaches, and its rivers; but above all, to fall in love with its magnificent people who undoubtedly deserve a much better fate than they have been handed.

A Bit of History:
From Columbus to Chávez

To understand what's going on in today's Venezuela, we must first trace back its origins. Venezuela was discovered by Christopher Columbus during his third voyage on August 2, **1498**, exactly 500 years before Hugo Chavez's rise to power. Columbus sailed the mouth of the Orinoco and the Paria Peninsula, where he decided to denominate our territory the "Land of Grace." Perhaps it was in this expression that there arose the premonition of what would later become our fate as a country dependent on oil revenue. Grace, as much in its use in religious language as its meaning in every-day language, designates something that is free or gratuitous, a favor where nothing is expected in return. Since the beginning of the **20**th

century, oil has been a fortune that is not exactly the product of our labor, but rather the result of a gratuity, a fortuitous event, a geological lottery, a shot in the dark that placed it directly beneath our feet. It may be said, perhaps generalizing but without straying too far from the truth, that for Venezuelans, wealth is not the product of effort, but rather "something" that "someone" distributes. In our case, that someone would be the state which, by law, owns all the oil.

The Spanish *conquistador* was in search of fortune. As Dr. Gil Fortoul suggests: "As long as gold existed, or at least the hope of finding it, the conquest could have no further objective."[2] In terms of wealth, Venezuela was not a particularly important territory as were some rich viceroyalties in the region; we were but a modest Captaincy General. During those three hundred years which Bolívar called "calm," the Spanish character shaped our identity, incorporating elements of Indians and African slaves. The crossbreeding of these three cultures is what ultimately led to our current way of life.

---

2   Gil Fortoul, José. "Sobre el elemento raza" in *Suma del pensar venezolano*. Fundación Empresas Polar, Ex Libris, Caracas, 2011, p. 139.

Let us now examine some of the traits of the Spanish character present in our cultural identity:

Improvisation. As Menéndez Pidal[3] points out in his introduction to *Historia de España* (History of Spain), the American conquest is, in many aspects, a series of "adventurous improvisations." The lack of a premeditated course has been one of the characteristics of our journey, a trait that seems to have exacerbated following independence: short-lived constitutions, arbitrary changes in course and government, and a defined underestimation of the most capable individuals. In our nations, intelligence and culture often become something of a stigma, a heavy weight for intellectuals to carry. There exists a telling dialogue between one of our first presidents, Dr. José María Vargas—civil, intellectual, renowned—and Pedro Carujo, one of the military officers who emerged triumphant from the War of Independence. Being reprimanded by Pedro, who had seized the president in his own residence to force his resignation, Vargas was yelled at from outside:

"Mister Vargas, this world is for the brave!"

"No," responded Vargas from inside. "This world

---

3 Menéndez Pidal, Antonio. *Historia de España*. Espasa Calpe, Madrid, 1947. Introduction, Volume I, Book 1, p. 29.

is for the just. It is the honest man, and not the brave one, that has and always will live happily on Earth and maintain a clear conscience."

A symptomatic dialogue of what awaited in the future: the struggle between an intellectual Venezuela—nearly always disregarded or at the service of the opposite Venezuela, that is a Venezuela of political adventurers with the force of arms and a lack of institutional respect which they erroneously call "courage."

Providentialism. Providentialism is characteristic to our way of life and keeps us expecting everything "from above;" in political terms, from those in power. *Caudillismo*[4] has been an integral element of daily life in Venezuela. More often than not they were military *caudillos* that, first sheltered by the glories of the conquest, then from independence a little later, and then from revolutionary triumphs much later on, became the overseers of our national fate. They were even present during the period of democracy that began in **1958** which, in our case, consisted of a democracy of civil *caudillos* subjected to the law and restricted in their capacities in accordance with democratic principles. Though this was a huge step forward, they were *caudillos* nonetheless, with

4   *Caudillismo* refers to a political-social system following Latin American independence from Spain that consisted in strong, charismatic leaders (*caudillos*) ruling over politically distinct territories.

authoritative slip-ups and ambitions of remaining in power that ended up damaging national institutions. Just when us Venezuelans thought that this phenomenon had been eradicated from our historical evolution and that we were finally moving on toward more rational forms of leadership, there came Hugo Chávez with the same characteristics seen in traditional *caudillos*: a military officer, self-oriented, arbitrary, and deeply anti-democratic, despite being—equivocally—the politician who has won the most elections in Venezuela.

Individualism. The conquest of our continent is, furthermore, a personal adventure of people who came here in pursuit of fortune and fame. Everybody was in search of immediate profit beyond the common good of the people and, on several occasions, they even worked against this common good. This explains why it is not the law that prevails, but rather privileges (etymologically deriving from the Latin *privus* and *legalis*, that is: "private law"). We often act just outside the limits of the legal system, if not completely against it. This idea that laws are enforced for pushovers and foolish people, or that they are an exquisite exercise of intellectuals in the service of powerful men who will have the final word anyway, has always been a weakness that has hindered institutionalization in this nation throughout the length of its history.

Cunning. For us, as well as for the Spanish *conquistador,* cunning is a value in the worst sense of the word: that of the capacity for manipulation and deception, the capacity to twist situations and take from them some personal benefit, the capacity to take shortcuts without regard to the potential detriment on others. It's something we Venezuelans usually term *viveza criolla,* "native cunning." To us, *vivo* (cunning person) is he who does not wait in line, he who profits from that to which he is not entitled, he who lies to take advantage of the masses, and, lastly, he who uses his wit for the purposes of corruption, fraud, and careful, profitable operations, often by treading carefully on the thin line that separates legality from illegality.

During the colonial period, the essence of the Venezuelan way of life was being established from the crossbreed between the three cultures that compose us. Traits from each of the three components of our initial settlement—the Indian, the slave, and the Spanish *conquistador*—have persisted in the modern expression of our national spirit. Let us go back to Gil Fortoul, who provides us a handful of clues:

"... from the Indian we get our love for independence and the hereditary hatred of caste privileges; from the African, at least in part, we get the energy we need for quick adaptation to the exuberant and wild nature [...] and from one or the other, the radical skepticism with which the less cultured part of the population often witnesses the bloody battles of volatile political sects [...] from the Spanish we get the lack of natural inclination toward industry, the weak spirit of initiative, the habit of expecting everything from the government, the passion for political intrigues, the taste for lively oratory [...] the untamable drive for war."[5]

The conquest was an act of war against the indigenous tribes that resisted, and Spanish superiority was thereby imposed. In contrast with other countries on the continent, our primitive inhabitants were not one of those vigorous cultures with the social and political organization that the Spanish came across in Mexico and Peru. In our case, it was basically a group of varying ethnicities that coexisted in what is now our national land. The *conquistador* enforced domination and imposed his own political model. The distribution

---

5   Gil Fortoul, idem.

of farmlands among the Spanish marked what would come to be the central element of our economy for many years: agriculture, especially coffee and cocoa plantations, the latter being reputed among the best in the world today. These first proprietors and their descendants constituted a caste, a social class that later became the "American Spaniards" —a privileged group in our case known as the *mantuanos*. This was an economically powerful class; it was politically subjected, however, to the power of the Iberic Peninsula, to the interests of the Spanish Crown, and to the authority of officials coming from the capital, oftentimes in conflict with one another. The feeling of self-determination, as is natural, finally emerged and gave way to some preliminary actions, such as those undertaken by Francisco de Miranda, who attempted various incursions on Venezuelan coasts with the aim of fostering the fight for independence. He failed in the face of apathy on behalf of his fellow citizens. Regardless, the Napoleonic invasion of Spain allowed the idea of separation from the Crown to bloom forcefully and this separation ended up materializing on April 19, **1810**.

Venezuelan independence was quite the complicated mix of political, social, and military proceedings. Our War of Independence from Spain was, for a great part of its pursuit, a civil war. The idea of separating from Spain was not necessarily a popular project, at least not in its initial stages. It was actually conceived under the wing of the ruling classes that, infused with principles from the European and American revolutions, wished to transmit the notion of freedom to the poor masses of the nation, masses which the ruling classes themselves were oppressing. These ideas, in the end, turned against their own initiators given that the ordinary population viewed them as their natural enemies and blamed them for all the abuses they were suffering. The fact that independence was pioneered by ruling classes of landowners, which also oppressed the population composed of slaves, Indians, small-time merchants, and farmers, made the ordinary population react with distrust and suspicion against the ruling class. The majority did not really understand what was under discussion and the adversaries of independence probably fought more for their own unique rights and freedoms than for the Spanish Crown, which was merely represented by a remote and unknown king. The War of Independence was hard, long, and extenuating with respect to the lives lost and the amount of resources employed. Venezuela, with Bolívar in command, took the lead in South American independence from the province of Caracas all the way to Upper Peru. Finally, after many rough years of victories and defeats, the outcome was a huge political project demanding the unification of the freed provinces into one single country: Gran Colombia (in honor of Columbus, the founder). However, it was very short-lived and quickly divided into several smaller republics resembling the organization attained from the Colony rather than the large, powerful nation that Bolívar had hoped for. He intended to secure the nation with the iron fist of a strong, centralized power, which produced contention and rejection regarding the constituent elements of federation. Thus, Venezuela was born in **1830** as a completely independent republic with nearly twice the land it has today.

Military *caudillos*, triumphant war heroes, took the course of the poor and indebted budding nation into their own hands. Although attempts were made to establish order and higher institutions, in reality they were operating in a self-oriented manner. José María Vargas, a medic and one of few civilians to poke his nose into political terrain, had a very rough presidency and ended up resigning. While generals became the new political class of landowners, discharged soldiers returning home to their families empty-handed dedicated themselves to the same thing they had been doing during the war: taking by force what they needed but didn't have. In the region of the *llanos*,[6] for example, the formation of armed groups dedicated to stealing livestock was not uncommon. For the poorest people and the commoners, independence brought few changes with respect to the unfair economic and social relations they had been suffering in the Colony.

During the **19th century**, communications in Venezuela were precarious, thus hindering the efficiency of political power. With the death of the indisputable superior authority, the *Libertador*, Simón Bolívar, all his subordinates

---

6   The Venezuelan *llanos* refers to the vast, natural flatlands that make up more than 25% of Venezuelan territory.

felt they were equally entitled and quarreled with one another for power. Two sides confronted each other: one side was made up of conservatives, which rather resembled liberals in many aspects; the other side was made up of liberals with a conservative ideology. Throughout Venezuela's history, political tags have had little or nothing to do with the true purpose hidden in the background: the pure and simple desire to seize power more than develop a political agenda. In fact, after the bloody Federal War, Antonio Leocadio Guzmán, one of the proponents of the federation, said the following:

> "I don't know where they got the idea that the Venezuelan people have love for the Federation when they don't even know what this word means. This idea came to me and several others who considered the following: assuming that every revolution needs a flag, and given that the Valencia Convention didn't wish to denominate the constitution with the 'federal' tag, we conjure up this idea; because if our adversaries, my dear sirs, would have said Federation, we would have said Centralism." [7]

---

7 Vallenilla Lanz, Laureano. *Cesarismo democrático y otros textos.* Edición Biblioteca Ayacucho, Caracas, 1991, p. 234.

This unveiling confession gives an account of the habitual use and abuse that has been made of ideological tags through Venezuela's history as a mechanism for political manipulation much more than acting as simple systems of ideas. It has been this way from the beginning up to the so-called "21st-century socialism."

There was no lack of revolutions or *caudillos* in the country by any means during the **19th century**: The Revolution of March, the Blue Revolution, the Restorative Revolution, the Rehabilitative Revolution, the April Revolution, and several others. Páez, the Monagas brothers, Antonio Guzmán Blanco, Cipriano Castro, "handless" Hernández, Falcón, and Ezequiel Zamora are some of the *caudillos* that distinguished this period, either by exercising their authority, fighting to bring it down, or both. As was to be expected, Venezuela came into the **20th century** in a miserable and indebted state, stripped of a large part of its territory due to its incapacity to defend itself legally or militarily. During the presidency of Cipriano Castro, the country was even cut off by its European creditors, Germany and England, in order to force the republic to settle the debts it had contracted.

General Juan Vicente Gómez, Castro's vice-president and close friend, turned out to be his successor. Gómez took advantage of a trip that Castro made abroad for a surgical operation by stripping the power right out of his hands and becoming the man who would stay in power for nearly three decades, the longest dictatorship the country had ever seen. He ruled with an iron fist, intolerance, and relentless war to all those who opposed him. He forcefully suppressed his opponents, who were murdered, jailed, tortured, or exiled over the desire to establish a modern democracy in Venezuela similar to those observed in the rest of the world. Above all, the brutality of these acts fell particularly on an entire generation of students known as the "Generation of 28" (**1928**) that rose up against the dictatorship from their universities. Juan Vicente Gómez governed the country with the same self-oriented approach with which he administered his estate, treating his fellow citizens as pawns.

Regardless, Gómez knew how to surround himself with loyal, talented, and bright intellectuals that provided his government with intellectual support and a reputation for enlightenment. At times, he would use them as substitutes in the exercise of power, temporarily putting them in charge while pretending to distance himself from the government. This gave off a sense of political rotation but, in reality, nothing was done without his consent, thus inspiring the following joke in popular humor: *aquí vive el presidente y el que manda vive enfrente.*[8]

Laureano Vallenilla Lanz was one of these prestigious intellectuals that justified Gómez's dictatorship with the famous thesis of the "necessary gendarme." Therein, he affirmed that, while our people were in the process of acquiring the capacity to govern themselves, they needed a strong government to raise them up and guide them with strict authority during that stage of "political infancy." This idea that the country needs a "strong man" seems to catch on again every once in a while among those of us who are so accustomed to personalist leadership in place of the solidity of laws and institutions.

---

8 Roughly translated as: "here lives the president, and the one in charge lives in front."

Gómez had other accomplishments as well, such as organizing the army which, since independence, was made up of so-called *montoneras*—groups of men with neither discipline nor uniform that served the *caudillo* in power, albeit in a disordered fashion. His government settled the country's foreign debt, built communication lines and routes—the labor force of which was made up of prisoners and incarcerated political enemies—that unified the territory and the government's control thereof. The organization of the army and the communicational control over the country saw the definitive end of the *caudillos* which, with their manpower and personal resources, had formed part of Venezuelan politics for many years. Regarding the economy, the most significant event during the reign of his government came particularly after **1918,** when oil displaced agriculture as the main economic source of income. In **1928**, Venezuela became the leading global exporter of crude oil.

The emergence of oil clearly marked the country's destiny all the way up to today. It turned us into a rentier nation dependent on a fortunate resource that is not the result of sustained effort, but rather price fluctuations in oil; a nation where the state plays a pivotal role in the distribution of revenue that was previously unheard of. However, this provoked several consequences: traditional economy was relegated to second place, especially that of agriculture and livestock, and masses of peasants began moving into the cities and oil production centers, thus precariously creating poverty belts on the outskirts of the cities or, in the case of the capital, in the surrounding hills outside of the reach of urban services. These poverty belts subsist even today, perhaps with greater deficits due to the reduction of national income and the lack of political plans to the effect. There also arose a powerful middle class linked to services, trade, and professional activities that the country's rate of growth demanded, as well as a business sector generated and sheltered by means of state income. Thus, Venezuela came to be considered a rich country given that it possessed the largest oil reserves in the world and was the main oil exporter for a remarkable period of time. This image stuck with us as much in the foreign view as in the vision we have of ourselves to the point that it has instilled deeply in our population the idea that access to wealth has to do solely with unequal distribution. As a consequence, the mindstate of expecting it all from the government surged forcefully and even the most modest individuals demanded their piece of the pie that they were watching others enjoy. If the less fortunate expected scholarships and subsidiaries, business owners would request soft loans and officials would seek opportunities for crooked deals and commissions.

Concurrent to this sudden explosion of wealth was the appearance of a new kind of dictatorship in the country: the modernizing dictatorship of Marcos Pérez Jiménez, who focused on constructing astonishing infrastructural works that gave the country the image of a modern nation that was beginning to stand out in comparison to the rest of its Hispanic American neighbors with respect to national development. The early attempts to establish democracy in the **20th century** were unsuccessful, either due to intolerance on the part of its advocates, who aimed to ostracize opposing parties and create a dominant party model, or due to the desire of the new military class, more prepared thanks to their academic formation and professional operation, to assume direct leadership over the country.

Having learned a rough lesson from the dictatorship of Pérez Jiménez, his government was brought down in **1958** thanks to a large-scale national agreement arising from a coalition of parties, students, trade unions, workers, the Church, and, obviously, the Armed Forces. Through this, a transition was established by means of a political pact (the long stigmatized Puntofijo Pact) that led to the period of greatest stability and national progress in the nation, with the occurrence of an efficient and lasting democratic model. This model was upheld by a broad consensus that gave rise to the longest-standing constitution in the history of the country: thirty-nine years, which, by our measure, is an eternity, given that Venezuela, just like Haiti, has the unfortunate record of being the country in the Americas with the greatest number of approved constitutions in its history. Growth, a product of the advent of democracy, was staggering on all levels of society with the stable and continuous access to goods and services that followed. The country saw a large number of European immigrants, a phenomenon that had already begun under the rule of Dictator Pérez Jiménez; education was now within reach of the majority of the population; the public health system eradicated endemic diseases that had decimated the population since colonial times; roadways were developed and modern highways were established; meanwhile, the process of industrialization was also gaining national momentum. The oil sector (up to that point in the hands of foreign companies) came to be under the direct ownership of the state, which established an essential company in Venezuela: PDVSA (Petróleos de Venezuela, S.A.), considered among the most important in the world. Political rotation among democratic powers with differing ideologies and philosophies took place in a perfectly normal manner. The guerrilla movement which Cuba sponsored in the 60s to help the communist revolution prevail throughout the continent made its peace and incorporated itself into political legality. The

Armed Forces were finally confined to their own domain—strictly military—as a rigorous professional body that is obedient to civil authority and non-decisive in political matters. During this time Venezuela attained its longest period of peace, its first century without civil wars.

However, by the end of the 80s the democratic process began to show signs of stagnation, incapable of amending faults and errors. Some rectification attempts were made, such as decentralization with support from the State Reform Commission, but they proved to be insufficient. Popular dissatisfaction turned into indignation in the face of occurrences such as:

- **Corruption**, or lack of transparency in the administration of public funds.
- **Increase in extreme poverty** and social exclusion for large portions of the population, while the rest of society averted their gaze without paying too much attention to the deterioration of the majority.
- **Reduction in oil prices**, always a hard blow to a state dependent on oil revenue and to a society governed by its profit.
- **Shortcomings**, lack of decisiveness, and corruption in the judicial branch.

In the end, a split was formed between elite political leaders and the population, the former being blamed for the people's misfortunes. This environment set in motion the idea of anti-politics, formed on the basis of the need for urgent change which demanded an "iron fist" to put an end to malfeasance in office. A group of left-wing officials in the Armed Forces had been plotting for some time; one of the leaders of the conspiracy, a commander, went by the name of Hugo Chávez.

Thus, the stage was set for the action to commence. The opportunity presented itself during the second presidential term of Carlos Andrés Pérez, who was re-elected into the government thanks to his popularity during his first term. This first term was marked by an oil boom that allowed him to run a populist government, though quite generous, during which a project known as *"la Gran Venezuela"* was developed. This project aimed to accelerate industrialization, eliminate unemployment, and establish plans for unmeasured growth and development which turned out to be unmanageable. It was, therefore, a time of surplus and increase in the average Venezuelan's quality of life. His second term, however, marked by low oil prices, aimed to amend the errors of the first. An austerity plan was initiated with the implementation of rigorous economic measures that baffled his voters and, given that no reasonable explanations were made and no compensation was given to those most adversely affected, protests arose and quickly degraded into shop looting throughout the entire country. These acts were strongly repressed by both the army and police force, though at a high cost of human life. This event marked the rest of his administration and created a favorable climate for the military uprising led by Hugo Chávez.

Though the attempted coup—rather bloody—proved unsuccessful, Commander Chávez gained fame and prestige that led to him being deemed worthy of consideration within Venezuelan politics. Having been imprisoned, he was pardoned by President Rafael Caldera in response to public pressure, as well as pressure from influential sectors of left-wing intellectuals, media outlets, and other figures in the country. Meanwhile, the crisis carried on and the idea of an "outsider" representing an alternative to the two traditional parties, both showing clear signs of exhaustion, began to gain increasing momentum.

Initially an advocate for electoral abstention, Chávez changed his strategy in **1998**, decided to run, and won the elections with a wide majority. Although his radical message was already creating strong resentment in large swaths of the middle and wealthy classes, the working class and the unsupported masses saw in his figure the *caudillo* that would glide soundly into the collective unconscious, the man who would recognize what the people lacked and who would be willing to defend them from economic and political power. Furthermore, he spoke the same language with the same authenticity as the working class.

The long, continuous, and fruitful development of what it means to be Venezuelan has been relegated by a history that puts heavy emphasis on political change and the actions of men in uniform. Thus, perhaps it would be appropriate to take a look at the history of national civility in Venezuela from a different angle. Venezuela was the nation that led Latin American independence, bringing with it novel ideas of unity. This ultimately produced exceptional men, not only in the military field but also civil heroes of great importance that left their mark, though they were very often excluded or underestimated. Next to Bolívar and Miranda, two universally-renowned names, we have figures such as Juan Germán Roscio, Andrés Bello, and José María Vargas, undeniable proof of the existence of distinguished thinkers on our soil—mere citizens committed to republicanism together with its laws and principles. Venezuela always shone brightly in the field of ideas and art: poets, musicians, renowned writers, distinguished scientists, and all sorts of entrepreneurs. A nation was progressively being developed, oftentimes having to swim against the current. In this country, we see a different image: a Venezuela of endeavor, work, and aptitude worthy of recognition. Being the immigrant-receiving country we are, especially since **1950**, an outstanding number of Europeans fleeing from the consequences of the war set up here, their new homeland, and established a new course for the country based on work and effort. In short, the human land-scape of a country is much more complex than that of the leaders who drive its political course.

This civil spirit of the Venezuelan nation picked up force and peaked with the establishment of democracy in **1958**. The country became an example for the rest of the continent to follow: a democracy that succeeded in changing its citizens' thoughts and actions. An intensive process of education expansion gave rise to a solid class of competent professionals, many being educated at the best universities in the world while new modern universities were being constructed in Venezuela. Likewise, Venezuela developed state-of-the-art communication methods, thereby rendering the country a pioneer in communicational innovation. During this time, Venezuela's infrastructure profile also changed with a series of modern construction projects, some being the first of their kind from a global perspective. The most significant change during this period, however, was the establishment of a new method of proceeding with matters in the country that classified dialogue and negotiation as having a preponderant role.

Venezuela approached the **20ᵗʰ century**, which for some began with the death of Dictator Juan Vicente Gómez in **1935**, with a sustained notion of advance and progress on every level.

On the other hand, while the idea of being a rich country—as a vision of our own conception—is a concept that has caused us such detriment since we place profit over work, it is undeniable that Venezuela is a country with unquestionable potential: a benign climate, fertile land, an abundance of water, navigable rivers, paradises ideal for tourism, kind and responsive people, etc. Although our economy moves at the pace of oil prices and we have yet to learn how to "plant petroleum," as suggested by Uslar Pietri,[9] on average, Venezuela is the Latin American economy with the greatest resilience and capacity to recover after having gone through a crisis.

---

9   This popular phrase by Uslar (*sembrar el petróleo → to plant oil*) first appeared in his article published in the Caracas-based newspaper *Ahora* on July 14, 1936. The phrase's intention is clear from this excerpt: "It is imperative to take advantage of the fleeting wealth of the current destructive economy to create sound, broad, and coordinated bases for the future progressive economy that will be our true declaration of independence. It is necessary to invest the bulk of the mine profits in aid, facilities, and incentives for national agriculture, husbandry, and industry. Instead of oil being a curse that will turn us into a parasitic and useless population, may it be a fortunate backdrop that permits the productive progression of the Venezuelan people toward exceptional conditions with its immediate wealth."

This arbitrary summary of Venezuela's history helps us understand, at least partly, what has befallen on us today as a consequence of long-standing grudges and inconsistencies, the resolutions of which have been postponed for far too long. On the brink of the 200th-year anniversary of the Venezuelan revolution for independence, the country found itself immersed in a brand-new revolution, as we are told, this time fighting for permanent independence and being led by a second *Libertador,* a parachutist in every sense of the word.

"Soft" Dictatorship

Hugo Rafael Chávez Frías, a mid-level serviceman, became the protagonist of the beginning of Venezuela's third century as a nation. His speech transcended the limits of Venezuela and became an emblem of hope for the most disadvantaged individuals both inside and outside the borders of his homeland. A skilled communicator, he knew how to captivate the masses with the simplicity of his emotionally-charged populist rhetoric, which was also laden with aggression toward those perceived by the people to be the enemies: the rich, the right-wing, imperialism, the bourgeoisie, the oligarchy, unbridled capitalism, etc. To this effect, all who opposed him were classified by him under at least one of these conditions. With Chávez there was no "on the fence;" you were either on his side unconditionally or you were considered an enemy.

His popular discourse, using a simple language quite often specked with the profanity of everyday speech, puns, and witty jokes, got the people riled up. Fed up with traditional rhetoric, they had been showing signs of increasing discontent. He offered a way to overcome all the evils that were causing their misfortunes: corruption, basic service crises, low wages, homelessness, lack of nutrition, lack of clothing, and a number of other difficulties shared by the people. He was capable of speaking for several hours without losing his audience's attention. For example, during the presentation of his reports and accounts before the National Assembly in **2012**, he gave a speech that went on for nearly 10 hours nonstop. By the end of it, he complained that he hadn't had enough time to summarize his year in charge. The age of Chávez was marked by rhetoric and propaganda much more than actual change in Venezuelan society. His inconsistencies, inequalities, corruption, and authoritarianism only accentuated in the end.

His appearance on the Venezuelan political scene began in the year **1992** when he headed a military coup against constitutional President Carlos Andrés Pérez. This military skirmish failed with a high cost of victims but Chávez, the coup leader, got a shot to fame, especially after his surrender message broadcasted live on Venezuelan television in which he stressed that the objectives had not been achieved "as of yet" and stated that new opportunities to achieve them would arrive soon enough. That "as of yet," with the suspense it implied, took root and became his slogan thereafter. The military coup produced sympathies in broad sectors of the population that saw the element of authority and order in the military figure that, according to many, was exactly what the country needed in that moment. Additionally, an intense campaign against the traditional parties, the failures accumulated by democracy, and the outstanding debts thereof in relation to the majority of the population established a framework of "anti-politics" which was also somehow hoisted up by some conservative sectors and media outlets.

Chávez could surf well in the tempestuous political sea at the time, but above all he succeeded in attaining popularity and was loved by many. Imprisoned along with his brothers-in-arms, he received a presidential pardon after two years of imprisonment and went on to found the Fifth Republic Movement. Although he initially promoted electoral abstention as a form of protest, he later decided to run in the elections under the guidance of left-wing political veterans and became President of the Republic in **1998**. Chavez's aims in the exercise of his power, which he clung to until his death in **2013**, varied in their nature, as we will try to present.

Refounding of the Country

Chávez clearly communicated the idea that he was ushering in a new era in Venezuela history marked by changes that would crush the old model which he contemptuously denominated the model of "rotten inner circles" or "*puntofijismo*," alluding to the well-known Puntofijo Pact that was signed at the downfall of Dictator Pérez Jiménez and which made democratic governability possible in the country for 40 years with political rotation between the social democratic party Democratic Action and the social Christian party Copei. Chávez accused this pact of having betrayed the masses at a pivotal point in our historical evolution, as well as having consolidated a capitalist, bourgeois democracy that served the interests of the United States of America and the national oligarchy that represented them in Venezuela.

The first government action taken by the new president was the summoning of a National Constituent Assembly to draft a constitution in accordance with the demands of the present. Chavism was backed by a broad majority in this Assembly, thereby permitting the drafting of a new constitution at short notice and its ratification with a clear majority by means of a popular referendum. This obsession of completely refounding the country led to other symbolic and significant actions: the name of the country was changed to the "Bolivarian Republic of Venezuela" in honor of the *Libertador*, Simon Bolívar, the pronunciation of which became commonplace in presidential language given that Chávez considered himself an heir and advocate of Bolívar's philosophy which, according to Chávez, inspired his government's work; the coat of arms was altered with the horse being changed from an untamed horse to a riding horse; an additional star was added to the 7-star flag in light of Bolívar's wishes that a star be added for the Guayana Province; the name of the currency was changed from *bolívar* to *bolívar fuerte* (i.e. "strong" *bolívar*) which, curious enough, came to be known as *fuerte* ("strong") right when three zeros were removed from the monetary amount. Thus, one thousand *bolívares*, by executive decision, became one *bolívar fuerte*.

Part of the refounding also comprised adopting a centralized model that would crush the decentralization practiced in previous years by his predecessors. Therefore, it was key that the majority of the 23 state governments that administratively make up Venezuela remained in the hands of his followers to avoid finding opposition regarding his desire to reverse what was a long-awaited conquest by the regions. Also, from an economic perspective, many changes were pushed forward that led to a centralized state with growing control and involvement in the economy. To Chávez's advantage, there was an extraordinary increase in oil barrel prices, which jumped from 9 to 130 dollars per barrel. The state established production checks; companies and productive lands considered to be strategic were expropriated and turned over to the public administration. Unfortunately, the government was not very efficient at managing them, thus leading to increasing levels of corruption, corporate bankruptcy, inefficient production, and countless other misfortunes. There came about a popular saying that Chávez was going to become a King Midas in reverse: everything he touched would turn into mud.

This inefficiency in the state's administrative capacity remained behind the cover of the exceptional increase in oil prices, providing a nearly unlimited spending capacity for the government and fostering a port economy. This favored importations at the expense of national industry, which was considered treacherous and stateless in the hands of adversaries to the regime whose sole purpose was to sabotage the so-called "Bolivarian Revolution." The Armed

Forces and the national oil company became distributors of the food supply imported by the government, thus creating a parallel infrastructure of marketing and distribution controlled by political authority.

A differential exchange-rate regime was introduced in the country and access to foreign currency was restricted. Needless to say, access to government-regulated currencies started to become a magnificent source of administrative corruption that has seldom been observed in global history, let alone Venezuelan history. Furthermore, the exchange model became a mechanism for political pressure on dependent private sectors. The divide between the black market and the official market has been kept in permanent expansion, causing the activity of importing with preferential dollars and calculating sale prices to the black-market dollar to flourish. A new class of millionaires with luxurious vehicles, mansions, yachts, bank accounts, and foreign properties quickly began to make their appearance. They were called *"bolichicos"* (i.e. Boli-boys) because their wealth depended on the Bolivarian Revolution's policies and their connections to power, but also because they were typically youngsters that didn't exceed 35 years of age.

The refounding of Venezuela ended up turning into an intensification of the evils that caused public discontent in the population that voted for Chávez: major corruption, both public and private, as well as deterioration of the government's administrative capacity. The administration was full of loyalists that were terribly qualified and lacked competency in the assignments to which they were entrusted.

While this was happening, Chávez continued to win every election he ran for. We may ask ourselves, "how can this be explained?" Part of the answer lies in the amount of resources at his disposal, in addition to his charisma and the popularity of his message. On the one hand, the country's institutions and economy were dismantled, yet on the other hand, extravagant wealth was reaching all corners of the country from the national treasury. Negotiating with the government and receiving shares of revenue became much more profitable than pursuing productive work, which faced increasing regulations and barriers. Simply traveling with preferential dollars became a tremendous trade: Venezuela earned the title of the only country where travelers could return from their trips with significantly more money than they had when they departed. Thus, for many, traveling proved to be more profitable than working and a number of notable fortunes were made from activities based on these preferential travel dollars. Venezuelan writer Mariano Picón Salas' quote, applied in the past during the dictatorship of Juan Vicente Gómez, defined this period well: as Venezuelans, we possessed the mentality of "let's live, keep quiet, and benefit." "My heart's an oppositionist, but my pockets are Chavist," declared many, evoking that native cunning, that ancient *viveza criolla*.

Chávez successfully amended his own constitution in order to eliminate re-election restrictions. The vast majority viewed Chávez's administration in a positive light. With Cuban assistance, he initiated a set of mandates and direct subsidy schemes for the population, which was starting to receive grants and support, as well as a low-cost food supply since it was possible for the government to sell products at a loss thanks to the increase in oil revenue. Also, he initiated healthcare programs that directly reached out to the neighborhoods with doctors coming in from Cuba and accepting Venezuelan oil as pay. The population was content; they got the sensation from Chávez that they were no longer invisible, they counted on him as defender of their rights, and, furthermore, they believed that Chávez was rounding up the sectors traditionally perceived as the root of their misfortunes. The commander's support during this period soon became unconditional to the point that there arose a famous quote through state advertising which, in the voice of a humble woman, went like this: "*Con hambre y sin empleo, con Chávez me resteo*" ("With hunger and no occupation, with Chávez I go all-in"). The population was receiving all kinds of aids and supports, but there was no structural policy to drag them out of poverty. The Minister of Education, Héctor Rodríguez, within the framework of a "campaign to eradicate poverty," made this telltale confession: "It's not like we're going to pull people out of poverty and lift them to the middle class just so they can become oppositionists." Hence, eradicating poverty wasn't exactly part of Chavez's plans. It was necessary to keep the people dependent on state relief which could then be used to buy political support.

Concentration of Powers

The other project that Chávez set in motion dealt with the growing concentration of power in his hands. Following the approach of Argentine sociologist Norberto Ceresole, an adviser of Chávez, he established a model by which traditional democracy was replaced with a new form of "democracy" that combined three defining factors: the army, the *caudillo*, and the people. Instead of building up institutions in the country, he called for the creation of a dominant civil-military party that would link the leader with the masses. To this end, representative democracy had to be dismantled in favor of a new and acclaimed form of "participatory and protagonist" democracy with immense mass mobilization.

Seeing that the *caudillo* was the highest expression of the people, interests between the two often got conflicted. Only the leader spoke on behalf of the people, only he truly knew what they needed, often even more than the people themselves. Therefore, according to this logic, anyone who opposed his intentions became a traitor to the people's common cause and was considered anti-patriotic and, naturally, an ally of the Bolivarian Revolution's biggest enemies: Yankee Imperialism—which, paradoxically, was and continues to be our biggest client—and the local Creole bourgeoisie at their service.

In order to enforce this political control, it was necessary to place the institutions at the commander's disposal. Thus, a personalist regime was implemented. Chávez began to appear on large billboards as a sort of "big brother" figure. His successive TV and radio appearances would go on for several hours each day. The state-run television network was exclusively dedicated to Chávez's political agenda and personal promotion, thereby excluding all dissident critical stances and, naturally, any oppositional presence. Private media outlets came to be faced with the perpetual threat of closure given that the state grants concessions to media outlets in Venezuela. Radio Caracas Televisión, a symbolic Venezuelan communications company with more than 50 years of uninterrupted broadcasting and a clear anti-Chavist orientation, was shut down in **2007** to serve as a warning and to instill fear and auto-censorship in the media.

The president took strict control of the prominent national oil company which, despite being state property, maintained a sort of administrative autonomy that prevented Chávez from running it entirely according to his own will. For this reason, during the regular broadcast of his Sunday program *Aló Presidente* in April **2002**, he drove 18,000 employees out of Petróleos de Venezuela, S.A. (PDVSA) while blowing a soccer referee's whistle and mimicking the pulling of a red card, ultimately stranding the workers in the streets with no recognition whatsoever of the labor rights guaranteed to them by law. From this point on, the company came to be known as a "redder than red company," as stressed by the new president appointed by Chávez. This alluded to the fact that nobody with an ideology differing from that of the ruling party, the symbol of which was the color red, could land a job there. The other central objective of Chávez was taking control of the Armed Forces. To complete the army-*caudillo*-people scheme, his brothers-in-arms would have to maintain unconditional loyalty toward him. The president came from the army and, in contrast with the provisions set by his withdrawal thereof, he wore his uniform frequently. He would rally up the soldiers with political speeches when visiting military bases. During successive purges he was progressively forcing the withdrawal of any officials he deemed not entirely loyal to his cause. By the same token, he fostered favorable conditions and privileges for members of the Armed Forces, from salary raises to their involvement in activities related to public administration and politics. The big business of food importation and distribution also fell under the control of the Armed Forces. Then began the discussion of a burning topic: based on allegations made from abroad, it appeared that some high-ranking officials may have been involved in the drug trade. In this respect, frequent reference was made to the "Cartel of the Suns," alluding to the suns adorning the epaulettes of Venezuelan generals.

This monolithic unit formed by Chávez and the Armed Forces was torn apart in **2002** when high-ranking officials went into revolt in the face of the violence unleashed in the streets of Caracas against the largest opposition-run protest the country had ever seen. It was said that these officials had asked the president to resign at the time, a fact that he later denied. That night, however, the Minister of Defense, General Lucas Rincón, announced on television: "He was asked to resign, to which he accepted." The fact is that the president was stripped from power for a couple of hours; when his loyalists enforced their authority, he took back the presidential palace. Many details regarding the April **2002** episode remain obscured without resolve: first of all, whether it was really an opposition-led coup, a power void, or just a ploy unfolded by the president on his brothers-in-arms to weed out the non-loyalists that would end up getting out of hand and turning against him. The case is that, following these events, presidential control of armed institutions became much tighter. The government's political slogans began to be used in military parades and proceedings, the Armed Forces began to call themselves "Chavist," and, in fact, it actually became Chávez's armed party.

Another distinguishing feature of the political control that Chávez ascertained in Venezuela was subjecting the remaining state powers to him. The Supreme Tribunal of Justice, the Comptroller General, the Public Defender (commonly known as the Ombudsman), the National Electoral Council, and all other independent state powers were put at his disposal. In the field of justice, judicial careers were over with and easily disposable provisional judges were instituted if necessary. The Comptroller General, in charge of looking after and maintaining administrative order, was also subjected to Chávez's guidelines without any sort of investigation being carried out with respect to the notorious cases of corruption that were taking place and were already in the public domain. Regarding the legislative branch, strategic errors of the opposition—which chose not to run in some parliamentary elections due to objections toward the electoral system—excluded it from the National Assembly such that the legislative branch fell entirely in the hands of the president. The same also happened to national bodies in charge of arranging legal proceedings, such as the Prosecutor General, which was employed to imprison adversaries. National bodies in charge of defending human rights, such as the Ombudsman, looked the other way when atrocities arose. Despite Chávez seeing a decline in opinion polls, the persecution of oppositionists and political prisoners continued to rise.

Because of its critical significance, control over the electoral process deserves special merit. Although, to be fair, Chávez always won by a wide margin in the booths, it is no less true that he was constructing himself a favorable system entirely under his control and subjected to his desires. This provided him with important advantages, such as the national body having limited control over campaigns headed by Chávez and his goons who made use of state funds and assets at their own discretion for electoral purposes. The electoral body also emitted exploitable regulations that allowed overrepresentation of the ruling party in areas with more supporters, thereby replacing populational representation with territorial representation wherever proved beneficial. The National Electoral Council did much more to harm and discourage voters who were in opposition: in **2004**, when the opposition requested a recall referendum as set out in the constitution, a list of oppositionists who signed against Chávez was elaborated. It was known as the "Tascón List," named in honor of the Chavist representative who endorsed it. This list served for seeking out oppositionists, denying them work in state-run institutions, discharging them from their jobs in the public institutions, and, above all, promoting the idea within the population that opposing Hugo Chávez was a bold move with a hefty price.

Thus, initially elected in **1998** for a presidential term of five years with no possibility of immediate re-election, Chávez ended up being re-elected as president on four different occasions, ruling for a total of 13 years. The final term of his presidency was cut short by his death.

His desire to stay in power was substantiated by the idea that Venezuela experienced a sort of second independence with him; Chávez was seen as the second *Libertador*. As a matter of fact, his image appears alongside that of Simón Bolívar in official events even today. He tried to convince society that the process he had started was irreversible and that there existed no other possibility for change beyond that which could be produced within his own party, now known as the United Socialist Party of Venezuela (PSUV). The phrase "they won't turn back" was a common slogan in his electoral campaigns that openly alluded to the impossibility of an opposition victory. Chávez reinstated in Venezuela the age-old concept of permanence in power typical of dictatorships of times past. He rejected any other possibility and denied those who thought otherwise. He coined derogatory terms to describe them, such as "squalid," "fascists," "big shots," "*pitiyanquis*,"[10] "oligarchs," and "rot," among others.

---

10 A derogatory term coined by Puerto Rican poet Luis Llorens Torres (1876-1944) to describe people who imitate the US lifestyle and reject their own origins. "*Piti-Yankees*."

Under his aegis, the militia and violent government-backed paramilitary groups began coming together with the task of confronting opposition-run protests with greater force. Community-based organizations known as "collectives" also emerged and defined themselves as groups "dedicated to promoting democracy, political groups, and cultural activities," something they actually tried to do in many cases. Nevertheless, some of them openly took the criminal course and continue to behave as such given the violent nature of their actions which, in many cases, included battery, theft, and even murder of their victims. All these groups benefit from tolerance for their actions, if not from direct state backing or protection and connivance from security agencies.

As can be guessed from the aforementioned, opposition to Chavism was met with great difficulties; not only the difficulties posed by the regime's increasing authoritarianism and intolerance, but also the limitations derived from the opposition itself. In the first place, the opposition was a minority during the lengthy stretch of time that it took Venezuelan society to awaken from the illusion instilled in them by the charismatic leader. To add to this, it was quite a challenge to bring together a cohesive group that would permit the establishment of a unity of purpose when time came to face the excesses of power. In the third place, many mistakes were made, such as, for example, refusing to run in the **2005** parliamentary elections, thus leaving the opposition completely outside of the political sphere during the time in which that legislature remained in office. This facilitated the government's ability to pass laws without any restrictions imposed on them whatsoever. It is also necessary to add that the opposition possessed no unity of purpose regarding how to confront Chávez. Although the opposition, and in particular the opposition parties, chiefly fought for a democratic way out of the situation oppressing Venezuela—as they continue to do in the present—there was certainly no lack of radical circles that sought forceful and short-term solutions, either through rebellion or a military coup, and even sought foreign intervention.

Provided, for the most part, that the anti-Chavist sentiment formed against his regime was not expressed as openly as it has been during the presidency of Nicolás Maduro, Chávez's political successor, the opposition was unable to pull together a unified, powerful, and effective strategy that would last. When Maduro finally became president, the reins of power were already tied down tightly under the strict control of Chavism. It was then that the opposition won the **2015** legislative elections with a wide majority.

So why do we refer to Chávez's time in power as the "soft" dictatorship? It is essentially due to the fact that, although it was clear that Venezuelan society was taking the fateful path toward authoritarian control on behalf of the "supreme and eternal commander," who acted in accordance with the long list of anti-democratic abuses and attitudes described herein, he was nevertheless backed by sufficient popular support. In the first place, this allowed him to carry on calling for electoral processes that he knew he could control. Secondly, given that the opposition was confined to the middle-class, professionals, the youth, academics, and intellectuals that, despite being numerous and active, did not comprise a clear majority of the population, they could be subjected by means of controlled repression and, above all, through the use of the violent collectives that headed counter-demonstrations on the same streets and on the same days that the opposition decided to hit the streets. Fear of dissidence was systematically and irrevocably instilled. In the end, Chávez's control over Venezuelan society was a slow, gradual process. Chávez often gave off the impression of falling back in order to attain his goals by an alternative route. Like in Swiss writer Olivier Clerc's fable about the boiled frog, he knew how to increase the temperature slowly and, with enough patience, ended up achieving all his objectives. By the time of his death, democracy in Venezuela was an empty shell.

With oil prices in decline, our nation in debt following a period of immense economic prosperity, the national productive apparatus in shambles, factories filing for bankruptcy, every economic sector struggling to stay afloat, and carrying the title of the country with the highest inflation rate and instability on the planet, the check for our binge arising from poor management of the surplus arrived at our doorstep. By this point, Chávez had already fled the scene; it was now up to his self-proclaimed "political son," Nicolás Maduro. It was his responsibility to assume the inheritance of a country exhausted after 13 years of conflict fostered by his "father," a country hungry for change and worn-out by the lack of food and medicine, as well as the abysmal economic crisis. The population, now with the majority in opposition, kept demanding an electoral resolution. However, in contrast to Chávez, who could rely on the votes of his supporters and initiated electoral proceedings, Maduro had begun to shut them down. Opposition to the regime, backed into a corner and with no way out, ultimately opted for rebellion and peaceful protests. Thus, the "hard" dictatorship commenced.

"Hard" Dictatorship

Before his final trip to Cuba where he was to continue receiving medical treatment for the cancer he was suffering from—an incident forever clouded in mystery and misinformation—and from which he would return solely to die in his homeland, Chávez made a statement on December 8, **2012**, that left an impact on the Venezuelan people: "If something were to happen that would incapacitate me from continuing my duties as President of the Bolivarian Republic of Venezuela… I implore you to elect Nicolás Maduro as President of the Bolivarian Republic of Venezuela." Many at the time questioned the motives for this surprising proceeding. Why Maduro? Why not Chávez's brother, Adán, for example, who instilled his left-wing ideas into Chávez during their youth and was an important political leader himself? Why not another member of the party with more charisma and a better track record? The explanation, according to some, lies in the fact that Nicolás Maduro was the only person in whose unbridled loyalty the president could confide in a party with internal conflicts and divisions that he was well aware of. Furthermore, perhaps it was based on the recollection of an incident by his predecessor, Cipriano Castro, who left power in the hands of Gómez—his close friend and vice-president—when he left the country in **1908** for Europe in search of medical treatment only to find that Gómez had stripped him of his government and forbid him from returning. Chávez sought somebody with unconditional and absolute loyalty that wouldn't seize his government if he were to miraculously come home cured. That person was Nicolás Maduro.

The commander's successor was a man who had been committed to left-wing ideas ever since his youth. He served in the left-wing organization *Ruptura*, founded by men prevailing from the armed struggle. Between **1986** and **1987** he studied in Havana, Cuba, at the

Ñico López School of Politics. Upon returning to Venezuela, he worked at the Caracas Metro company as a bus driver where he became associated with union work. Maduro met Chávez when the commander was incarcerated, appointed himself to his agenda, and became part of his political movement. Concurrent with Chávez's victory, Maduro later became a representative of the National Constituent Assembly, representative of the National Assembly, president of the National Assembly, Minister of Foreign Affairs, and Vice-President of the Republic. Since Chávez didn't manage to swear himself in for his last term, Maduro took charge as "acting president," thereby disregarding the provisions set out in the constitution which declare that the President of the National Assembly must assume the role until new elections are held. Given that the constitution expressly prohibits anyone who performs the functions of vice-president to run as a presidential candidate, the Supreme Tribunal of Justice produced a *sui generis* interpretation according to which, upon re-election, Chávez could remain in charge even without being formally sworn in; therefore,

Maduro could be acting president even without his formal designation as vice-president for the new term in accordance with the laws. As José Tadeo Monagas presumably stated in the **19th century**: "In Venezuela, the constitution serves all purposes." Thus, Maduro was vice-president of the previous government, acting president of the following government, and a presidential candidate.

The presidential elections were held in April **2013**. Henrique Capriles Radonski was the opposition candidate. These were perhaps the most improper elections in all of Venezuelan history due to the amount of resources employed by Maduro and the obligatory chaining of media outlets to transmit the official candidate's messages at the unrestricted expense of state funds, amid other despotic acts that exceed any other similar act observed in the past, including those committed by Chávez himself whose abuses of power were already commonplace. The opposition candidate reported 3,500 irregularities before the electoral body over the course of the process, a prime example being the fact that opposition parties were blocked from voter registration auditing. To add fuel to the fire, the results were practically a tie: Nicolás Maduro won **50.61%** of the votes and Henrique Capriles Radonski won **49.12%**. The latter disregarded the National Electoral Council's report and requested an election recount that was subsequently denied.

In light of all the aforementioned, as well as the doubts concerning his double nationality given that he was supposedly born in the neighboring country of Colombia and nobody has viewed his original birth certificate to date, Maduro assumed the highest office in the Venezuelan nation in the year **2013** under the guise of the successor of Chávez's work and claiming to be his "son" and political heir. A curious folkloric detail: on one occasion, he even affirmed that Chávez appeared before him in the form of a little bird in a chapel and that he spoke to him in his unique and distinctive chirp. Maduro constructed a myth based around the memory of his predecessor, who came to be known as the "supreme and eternal commander." He effectively became an unyielding advocate of Chávez's policies in both the economic realm as well as the political landscape in spite of the fact that some sectors within the Chavist system started accusing Maduro of deviating too far from the path and even betraying the commander's legacy. In the economic realm, he maintained tight state control and did nothing to resolve conflicts with the productive sectors, the expropriation of businesses, and the permanent threat hanging over their heads. The economic blunders following so many years of ineffective policies finally started to catch up to the country. Faced with this, Maduro, far from rectifying the situation, refused to compromise in regard to his economic policy and accused "stateless bourgeoisie in alliance with Yankee imperialism" of promoting the so-called "economic war" which aimed to bring down the revolution and facilitate foreign invasion. Price regulations were maintained amidst a rising inflation process while imported products were infinitely cheaper thanks to the magnificent controlled dollar subsidy. Constant wage raises were announced by the president who proclaimed himself "the worker's president." Thus, he aimed to run as an advocate for the working class when, in reality, the constant raises have proven to be compelling evidence to wage inadequacy and the lack of efficiency regarding the measures adopted in this respect.

In the political landscape, Maduro exacerbated the intervention and control over other state powers. Before losing the elections in the National Assembly in **2015**, to which the opposition showed up solidly united and obtained a crushing victory, the governing party took advantage of the few days remaining in the outgoing National Assembly (the majority of which was Chavist) to designate a new Supreme Tribunal of Justice of audacious partisan composition that was entirely in favor of the government. In this way he violated the terms, procedures, and requisites established in the constitution, subverted procedures and regulations to the effect, and even designated representatives from his own governing party as judges—with immense cynicism. Thus, the highest court in the nation was filled with judges that were not only loyal, but openly subjected to the desires of the regime to the point that the Prosecutor General condemned the null and void nature of the designation given that it was never approved by her as demanded by constitutional rule.

Maduro copied the aggressive and popular rhetoric style of his political father, though clearly with neither the same emotion nor communicational capacity of his predecessor. His popularity started to plummet rapidly. The fall in oil prices and the abysmal management of the once-flourishing oil industry—which gave rise to increasing deterioration of its productive capacity—undermined the state's ability to distribute resources and finance the populism that had yielded political dividends during the final years of Chávez. A country whose government rendered it dependent on subsidized importations in order to sell products for less than what they were worth began to see problems with the shortage of foreign currency. Continued exchange control, in addition to the ever-increasing gap between the controlled dollar and the black-market dollar, made corruption much more tempting. The economic crisis that had already begun to dawn with Chávez exacerbated: restricted production capacity in national industry coupled with a drop in importations, price controls, and further adverse economic actions resulted in a product shortage, constant price increases accompanied by the highest inflation rate on the planet, and never-ending lines of people in search of regulated products in the supermarkets. Consequently, this sparked a black market for the resale of controlled goods known as *bachaqueo*, alluding to a remarkably large, red ant in South America called a *bachaco* that is capable of transporting enormous amounts of food.

Imported medicine also began to disappear from pharmacies and national laboratories were either leaving the country or shutting down due to the lack of base materials and the absurd sale price regulations that were far less than the production costs for the medicine, much of which ended up disappearing while the laboratories shut down or worked at minimum capacity. In turn, this dealt a hard blow to the pharmaceutical industry in Venezuela, so much so that they speak of an **85%** shortage of medicine. If, in addition to this, we consider the persistent deterioration of public services, particularly state healthcare services with underpaid doctors abandoning the country in search of new and improved paths for their professional practice, the lack of maintenance and renovation of medical equipment, the lack of healthcare improvement policies and new hospital construction, and the reappearance of endemic diseases that had practically been eradicated in the past but have now returned due to neglect in prevention policies, we find that we are faced with a truly desolating image in the Venezuelan healthcare sector.

The decline of living standards started to make its mark in an increasingly rapid manner. Thousands of citizens jumped into the migration process that had already begun under Chávez (something like three million emigrants is often mentioned) while a number of others remained without employment and got involved in the informal economy or the trendy new business scheme—the *bachaqueo*. People who rummage through waste collection zones for leftovers of food have become a regular part of our urban landscape. Infant mortality has begun to reach alarming numbers, even according to statistics by the Minister of Health, Dr. Antonieta

Caporale, who was removed from her position in May **2017** for daring to publish these reports on the official Venezuelan Ministry of Health website in a nation where official performance numbers disappeared long ago. In her report she spoke, among other topics, of a **30%** rise in infant mortality in **2016** compared to the previous year, a **65.79%** rise in maternal mortality, and a **76.4%** rise in cases of malaria.

All that we have been discussing negatively contributed to some of the other grand problems that have overwhelmed the Venezuelan people in recent years: uncontrollable citizen insecurity, an increase in crime, and dramatically cruel acts by delinquents and criminals against their victims. To better control prisons, the government negotiated with gang leaders with the purpose of ensuring order in the prisons to defuse the rampant violence. This resulted in a new authority within the detention facilities: the so-called *pranes*. They have something of a feudal lord position, controlling vast areas of the country and directing criminal operations in those regions from within the prisons where they handle money and military weapons and, in some, even manage recreation centers and clubs. In addition to them, some of the collectives escalated their own acts of violence. Internal divisions in the governing party also affected them following the death of Chávez. As Diosdado Cabello, leader of the ruling party, affirmed openly and unequivocally: "Chávez was the retaining wall for all those crazy ideas that occur to us." Thus, the Venezuelan citizen is subjected to two forms of violence: violence by criminal delinquents and violence by armed groups controlled by the government. Despite the fact that the latter has a political character, it has also displayed itself in the form of criminal and aggressive acts.

It is not difficult to infer that with this national state of widespread deterioration, delineated herein, rejection against Maduro's administration continued to increase. According to opinion polls, the population that expresses itself as anti-Maduro now makes up the clear majority. The establishment of a united opposition block facilitated the coordination of a more agreeable and coherent opposition agenda. In response, Maduro scaled up the persecution and repression of opposition leaders, many of whom were incarcerated starting with the emblematic opposition leader Leopoldo López following the February **2014** protests that he led. Hundreds more were imprisoned, followed by thousands as a result of the **2017** protests. Maduro far surpassed his "father" with respect to his escalation of intolerance and removal of options that would strip the power from his hands. To start with, he made electoral solutions impossible given that he had already lost the people's sympathy. Backed by the absolute control of the electoral body, Maduro continued suppressing electoral processes established in the constitution, such as the election of governors based on set terms and, especially, the possibility of performing a recall referendum that the constitution sets aside for the presidential midterm and in which the population in opposition had entrusted all their hopes of an immediate and constitutional way out. To this respect, Maduro's statements were blunt and completely without restraint. In November **2016**, he said: "Those people (the opposition) will proceed no further here, neither for good nor for evil, neither with votes nor with bullets will they ever enter Miraflores (the seat of government); they shall not return..." In June **2017**, he went even further with this threat: "If Venezuela were to plunge into chaos and violence and the Bolivarian Revolution were to be destroyed, we would go into combat. Never shall we surrender and, what can't be accomplished with votes, we would accomplish with arms."

Aside from shutting down electoral solutions, Maduro attempted to reverse the progress made by the opposition through their vote and he eventually succeeded. Utilizing the Supreme Tribunal, which was absolutely subjected to his will, he had them cite the National Assembly, composed primarily of opposition members, for contempt of court in January **2016**, just after the election in December of the previous year. The highest court in the nation attributed some of the functions of the National Assembly to itself while simultaneously reversing all the decisions made in the heart of the Assembly time and again. Finally, some very violent members of his party entered the National Assembly's head office by force and beat up several representatives while the National Guard, responsible for safeguarding facilities in the Federal Palace, watched complacently. The regime found itself operating blatantly outside of the constitutional framework and employed force as its sole support.

The shutting down of all electoral options, in conjunction with the severity of the crisis, the reigning violence, and the growing intolerance on the part of the government with respect to dissident protests, pushed opposition leaders to develop much more robust actions, such as peaceful protests that overflowed every city and street in the country. In some cases, these even proved to be out of hand to the leaders who initially fostered them. These protests, now known by some as "the Venezuelan spring," began in April **2017** and went on for four months with marches and rallies being performed practically every day. The government responded with brutal repression by the National Guard and the regime's political police, known as SEBIN.[11] The unlimited and

---

11 SEBIN stands for the *Servicio Bolivariano de Inteligencia Nacional* (Bolivarian National Intelligence Service).

disproportional use of force, including the use of weaponry by the police force, resulted in more than 150 deaths including many caused by the use of firearms. Additionally, thousands of cases of extrajudicial detention were recorded. Other human rights violations, such as torture, mugging of protestors by police, the use of prohibited substances, weapons, and various types of projectiles (marbles, screws, metal rod fragments, etc.), put the brutality and repression with the aim of containing citizens on the spotlight. These acts are meant to instill fear and dissuade the population from taking to the streets. The victims have chiefly consisted of young people who are much feistier and more reckless when it comes to approaching areas of stricter control and police aggression at the forefront of demonstrations and rallies. Thus, the regime revealed its darkest side, that is, its capacity to exercise a level of repression over the population that lacked any control whatsoever. The premeditated, systematic practice of brutally eliminating oppositionists had not been observed since the times of the cruel dictators Gómez (**1908-1935**) and Pérez (**1950-1958**).

The regime demonstrated that it is willing to do whatever it takes to stay in power. Not only will it take actions that lie outside of the legal framework, but it will also succumb to stepping outside the boundaries of human rights and, indeed, any notion of humanity whatsoever.

Faced with the worsening gravity of the country's internal situation, as well as the evident loss of governance, President Nicolás Maduro filed a proposal which, according to him, was conceived as the sole method of guaranteeing peace amidst the widespread protests of **2017**: the creation of a Constituent National Assembly to draft a new constitution. The proposal received negative feedback throughout the country. It didn't go well with the followers of Chavism given that it implied a change in the **1999** constitution which, based on the discretion of the "supreme and eternal commander" while he was still alive, was considered "the greatest in the world." Regarding the opposition, the proposal was met with outright rejection. Among the various reasons for their refusal, the one that stood out most dealt with the election methods suggested by Maduro: there would be no direct, discrete, and universal suffrage for the election of constituent members, but rather they would be elected by sectors divided in accordance with Maduro's criteria such that only his loyalists could find their way into the National Constituent Assembly. As if this weren't enough, the new constitution was not to be subjected to any sort of approval on behalf of the voters by means of a referendum as established by Venezuela's standing Magna Carta. The perception floating in the minds of the majority of the population is that the National Constituent Assembly will be used to further solidify the dictatorship and remove the legal constraints that continue to persist in the executive branch. The deliberations of the National Constituent Assembly are without deadlines or restraints and Maduro already indicated that he has devised some laws which he plans to submit for consideration to the provisional Assembly, one of them intended to establish greater controls over the economy.

On the other hand, the opposition responded by persisting with rallies and protests in the streets, in addition to new forms of protesting known as *trancazos*. These consisted in rounding up locals, which, by the way, was carried out in a highly efficient and organized manner, and blocking off main arterial roads in the city based on a fixed schedule. In light of the activities being dissipated throughout the entire city (and, indeed, throughout the entire country), it became increasingly difficult for officials to repress the population. The locals remained near their homes so that they could withdraw with ease. Regardless, there have been cases of excessive repression against neighborhoods and buildings. For example, they tossed tear gas bombs and even shot through windows without any warning to the civilians who live there, including children and elders. They raided homes without court orders, they destroyed private property, and they detained individuals without an arrest warrant.

Amidst rising repression, the institutional blockade of the National Assembly and even of the Prosecutor General, Luisa Ortega Díaz, a longtime loyalist to Chávez now turned the only authority to condemn the remaining arbitrary state powers under Maduro, the opposition decided to hold a referendum on July 16,

2017, to enable the population to express their desires with respect to changing the political system practiced in Venezuela. Three inquiries were to be submitted during the referendum: first, to express rejection or acceptance toward the National Constituent Assembly summoned by Maduro; second, to request the Armed Forces and state officials to commit themselves to defending constitutional order; and third, in regard to the people's will to revamp public authorities by means of elections and the formation of a government dedicated to national unity.

The referendum was conducted with remarkable success, despite the heavy blockade imposed by the government in various ways, such as making it impossible for media outlets to emit information regarding the progress of the referendum, impeding the spreading of awareness and promotion under the threat of being shut down, and even direct action by violent groups intent on sabotaging the ballot. The actions carried out by these groups led to the death of a nurse, Xiomara Scott, who was standing in line to vote in the low-income residential zone of Catia in Caracas, as well as numerous

other injuries. Chavism is particularly suscepti-
ble to opposition protests in areas with the poorest sectors of the population. But despite the fact
that the inhabitants of these areas were offered
to vote in less risky parts of the city so they
wouldn't be under control by these groups, these
people, courageous and determined, preferred
to vote in their own localities. 7.5 million citizens participated in the referendum and casted a
98% vote against the convening of the National
Constituent Assembly. This was indeed quite
an extraordinary turnout considering that the
procedure was organized by the citizens themselves in a period of 15 days and with significantly less seats than the amount used in electoral processes.

The government, however, carried on
with the election of the National Constituent
Assembly, formed on July 30, **2017**, as planned.
It was only attended by candidates who support-
ed Maduro's regime. For its part, the National
Assembly conducted sessions and made decisions that, in practice, were not respected by
any of the public authorities which were under
the executive branch's control. This was done

without any support from representatives of the governing party who ditched the sessions ever since Parliament was cited for contempt of court by the Supreme Tribunal.

Maduro's government, in a clever political maneuver, decided to hold the regional elections that had been postponed since **2016**. This was done directly after the allegation made by the company Smartmatic, which provided its services to the National Electoral Council. In August **2017**, Smartmatic warned about the confirmed rigging of votes during the National Constituent Assembly election. This occurrence put the opposition in a harsh dilemma: on the one hand, not attending regional elections even though they could count on enough votes to win would be equivalent to delivering all the governorates in the country to the ruling party on a silver platter; and on the other hand, participating in them would act as a cover for the fraudulent voting procedure and therefore recognize a government that has been condemned both nationally and internationally for acting outside the framework of constitutional order as legitimate. The opposition opted to participate and a good portion of the population in opposition saw this as an unjustifiable betrayal. The opposition, which had successfully formed a solidary group, was once again split. In view of the unexpected decision by the opposition to attend regional elections, the regime unleashed new strategies: some of the opposition leaders could be rendered ineligible.

Thus, Maduro ended up achieving his objectives. First off, he divided the opposition, which he discredited by saying that they held secret conversations with him in order to reinforce the image of betrayal attributed to them by so many. Second, he scattered the opposition's capacity to protest which, after four months of being repressed and failing to achieve any of their proposed objectives, found itself in a state of complete exhaustion. Consequently, this made the opposition feel unrepresented by a form of leadership that many believe has settled their battles.

Nonetheless, in spite of the discouragement instilled in the opposition by the government after months of street protesting, they did in fact accomplish some important goals and

Nicolás Maduro's regime was left out in the open on an international level with respect to its conduct in its disregard for the legal framework, its actions that overstep the boundaries of the constitution, and the systematic human rights violations carried out during protests.

On the other hand, aggression against political leaders and figures of the opposition increased exponentially. Confiscation of passports at immigration checkpoints in Venezuelan airports turned into a sort of *de facto* method of prohibiting people from leaving the country. Mayors and governors are often harassed and some of them have even felt the need to flee the country to avoid being detained. The release of political prisoners has not yet materialized. Councilman Carlos García, representative of the Justice First party in the municipality of Guasdualito in Apure State, died in SEBIN's solitary cells after being denied medical attention for a stroke he suffered in August **2017**, just one month before his death. Many other prisoners require emergency medical attention, but they do not receive it. General Isaías Baduel, a longtime friend and ally of Chávez who was instrumental in his return to power in April **2002**, endured something of a kidnapping by authorities. His family spent weeks bearing no knowledge whatsoever of his whereabouts, the detention facility where he was being held, or whether he was even still alive.

The stark actions taken against Maduro's government by Prosecutor General Luisa Ortega Díaz, a longstanding associate of the regime, as well as the unexpected accusations of cases of corruption that she had kept up with in her records, caused the National Constituent Assembly to dismiss her and she was forced to flee the country to avoid incarceration. Tarek William Saab, who went from being Ombudsman to State Prosecutor General, was appointed in her place. The dismissed Prosecutor General began to conduct her reports on cases of corruption and human rights violations carried out by the regime from abroad.

At the time of this book's publication, the outcome of Venezuela's current situation remains unclear. Resolute statements made by world leaders on the country's situation radiate from the United Nations General Assembly where they place Maduro's government in a spotlight that demands attention and global alarm. US President Donald Trump speaks of hard-hitting actions against Maduro's government on behalf of his country. Economic sanctions aside, he does not rule out the possibility of military sanctions. Together, these provide the Venezuelan president with a new arsenal of excuses to justify the political, economic, and social crisis generated by the incompetence of his own government. Now, he is accusing Trump of calamities that we have spent over a decade suffering from. Experience with Cuba reveals that, in the end, embargos and other unilateral actions related to force only strengthen left-wing dictatorships.

Venezuela currently finds itself at quite a complicated crossroads with a growing climate of uncertainty taking hold of the population. Luis Vicente León, director of one of the most prestigious research and analysis firms in Venezuela and a reputable speaker on themes related to economics and political analysis, envisions three possible scenarios:

1) The government will remain in power and the country's deterioration will persist and accentuate. To this effect, the government will be forced to escalate repression and openly involve the Armed Forces. Instability will prolong as a result of upholding the economic policies that caused the crisis in the first place. It's a scenario of national subjugation and the dismantling of any and all opposition groups.

2) Protests will get completely out of hand and expand to the point that no manner of repression can be efficiently carried out. They would no longer be simply protesting in the streets, but everywhere in the country. This would paralyze the nation, thereby rendering it impossible to govern and leading to the following scenario.

3) The internal fracture of Chavism and the pursuit of an agreement to negotiate a transition that would guarantee the survival of outgoing actors and the institutional reorganization of Venezuela.

At the present moment, the first scenario is in full swing.

Epilogue

The situation in Venezuela is difficult to understand. To the rest of the world, it seems inexplicable why it's so challenging for us to find an electoral or negotiable way out, such as the Venezuelan opposition aimed to do. This has not yet occurred for one fundamental reason that is necessary to emphasize crudely and plainly: the reigning political regime has come to be seen as openly criminal on both a national and international level. The country's institutions are in the hands of people accused of various types of crimes: corruption, human rights violations, ties with terrorist groups, drug trafficking, etc. For this reason, the customary standards reserved for political negotiation in Venezuela have not seemed to function because, for one of the conflicted sectors, negotiation does not consist of a way to establish accords by means of concessions, but rather a strategy to buy more time, radicalize even more positions, and, finally, survive the only way they know how: by ensuring permanence in the control of power. Chávez conducted a process in which he surrounded himself with unquestioning loyalists, though they were incompetent and had a limitless appetite. Loyalty coincided with tolerance, a lack of checks and balances, and lawlessness which found itself escalating into a never-ending spiral of corruption. Benito Juárez's advice stood firm: "Everything for my friends, the law for my enemies;" because in our society, laws are instruments for vengeance and repression more than parameters for civil harmony. With Chávez gone, his allies divided into separate warring factions that were solely unified by the idea of staying in power at any cost to avoid the national and international sanctions already announced to a growing list of officials. Without a doubt, collusion was the main cohesive factor that brought together followers of Chávez.

A politician understands that power is gained and power is lost and that, in a democratic society, whoever gains it doesn't gain it all and whoever loses it doesn't lose it all; that's what the democratic game is all about. But when crime takes the throne, the loss of control incurs risks that are unacceptable to the ruling party. Thus, in situations of this nature, one is willing to commit any illegal act and as many human rights violations deemed necessary to keep power under seizure. The most aggravating aspect of the situation is that the absolute incompetence of the president to guarantee a minimal level of governance in running the country has turned Venezuela into what is known in political science as a "failed state:" a state whose government is unable to exercise control over the country, a state which does not possess a monopoly of the legitimate use of physical force, given that it transformed security forces into armed groups that overstep the boundaries established by law, and a state that is incapable of supplying basic services that the people need, guaranteeing economical operation, and observing the rule of law. Consequently, all of this places us outside the sphere of democratic nations.

Cuba, together with Bolivia and, more hesitantly, Nicaragua, comprise the few supporting allies remaining for the dictatorial regime in Venezuela. Cuba is attributed with having control over some areas of government in the country and the president makes frequent visits to the Caribbean island. It is said that Cuban intelligence services operate freely in Venezuela and that they play a direct role in the Armed Forces, as well as the civil and land registers. The Minister of Defense receives medical treatment in Cuba, as do all other high-ranking officials that require any sort of treatment. Even President Chávez was tended to in Havana; his state of health was a jealously guarded secret and our Head of State, who was making decisions and signing decrees from his hospital bed, was at the mercy of foreign authorities in a country from which he returned unconscious. To this day, we are still unsure if the decisions made from over there were actually his. That Venezuela supplies free oil to Cuba, and that the island has a keen interest in watching the situation in Venezuela persist, is a public and notorious fact.

The theme of drug trafficking and the manner in which it has been implemented into the highest realms of political and military authority is another culminating point when addressing the Venezuelan situation and has already given rise to investigations and international sanctions, such as the arrest in the United States of the nephews of the president's wife, denominated by him as the "first combatant." The "narco-nephews," as they are ironically known, were detained in Haiti by US intelligence agencies after a flight in which they were supposedly traveling to discuss matters related to selling drugs. The private plane they were flying in took off from "terminal four" in the Caracas airport in Venezuela, a terminal reserved exclusively for the President of the Republic. Thus, Venezuela has been denounced as a "narco-state." According to experts on the subject, this situation originated in the relationship, backed by Chávez, between our Army and Colombian narco-guerrillas. It is said that they facilitated activities by Colombian rebels in Venezuela to maintain sources of funding. From there, high-ranking civil and military officials started to get involved in the business.

These acts have been condemned by important US politicians, such as Senator Marco Rubio, and renowned figures in Latin America, such as Costa Rican ex-president and Nobel Prize winner Oscar Arias.

As a consequence of everything stated herein, Venezuela has entered an ungovernable terrain with an electoral system that has been openly questioned and a government that is incapable of negotiating for reasons already exposed. To add to that, there is a severe humanitarian crisis in full swing with malnutrition and lack of healthcare topping the list, not to mention the fact that Venezuela has the highest inflation rate and crime rate in the world. Furthermore, the country is constantly ravaged by the existence of armed paramilitary troops controlled by the government, an Armed Forces assembly turned military wing for the governing party, and a rising number of desperate citizens that see emigration as their only way out.

Venezuela is, without a doubt, coursing through one of the bleakest periods of its history. There is no doubt in our minds that we will escape this situation, though at a high cost of human lives and prosperity. For those who "rule," the costs of losing power are infinite. They know that if they abandon their posts, they will be lost both inside and outside the country. The questions that arise are as follows: Just how long can a failed state stay afloat? How much longer will the population put up with dying from starvation or untreated illnesses? How many more innocent civilians will be forced to fall in order to subjugate a population that has rebelled peacefully, yet compellingly? These are the concerns and apprehensions that float aimlessly around us.

We must not conclude with a hopeless vision. If you have made it this far, my dear reader, it is because you hope, as much as the author of these pages, for a happy ending to this story; and Venezuela deserves one. It is a gorgeous country, both physically and spiritually speaking. Spreading awareness of what is happening here is part of our mission, as is reconstructing the idea of international solidarity and global commitment toward prosperity.

No nation is so distant to the point that it is unable to affect your daily life in some way.

But aside from that, it may be that threats similar to those that struck Venezuela so hard are being forged in the political situation that you find yourself in. Warning against anti-politics, simplistic demagogy, and destructive populism is part of our commitment. Politics are, and must remain, a noble task, a responsibility to all of humanity, to the well-being of the most humble, and, above all, a commitment to a life of respect and tolerance, a life of solidarity, honesty, and benevolence, because, as the Spanish mystic San Juan de la Cruz[12] would say: "At the evening of life, we shall be judged on our love," and politics would have to be the quintessential exercise of love.

Aside from the terrible sufferings we have related briefly and concisely herein, sufferings which have ravaged Venezuela, our nation continues to be one of talented and admirable people, of artists, of culture, of natural wonders, and of the same desire for progress that attracted so many people in times past. Venezuela has huge reserves of optimism, ingenuity, and even

---

12 Often known in English as Saint John of the Cross

democracy and freedom in its collective spirit. There are many things we must change in how we face our own destiny after this trying lesson. That clash between civilization and barbarianism that Mr. Rómulo Gallegos discussed in his famous novel, *Doña Bárbara*, continues to distinguish our fate. History's pendulum will soon tilt toward the side of civilization, that we can bet on. In the meantime, returning to Gallegos, we shall continue to be a "land of open horizons, where a good race of people loves, suffers, and waits."